NOT A MONSTER

What We Get Wrong About Sociopathy

Channa Bromley, PhD

Not a Monster

eBook ISBN: 978-969-9293-10-8
Paperback ISBN: 978-969-9293-11-5
Hardcover ISBN: 978-969-9293-12-2

Praise for Channa Bromley, PhD

"Dr. Channa is creating a ripple effect that will inspire generations of women to break free from toxic patterns, heal deeply, and thrive both personally and professionally."

— Billboard Lifestyle

"In a world where challenges can either define or destroy, Dr. Channa Bromley stands as a beacon of transformation and empowerment. Once caught in a harrowing cycle of trauma, addiction, and self-destruction, she made the courageous decision to rewrite her story."

— The Hollywood Times

"In an era overflowing with surface-level advice and emotional clichés, Dr Channa stands apart as one of the most intriguing minds in modern relationship strategy. A global Relationship Strategist with an unconventional, precision-driven approach, she merges psychological depth with structural design to engineer the subconscious patterns that shape how people love. Her work does not resemble therapy, nor does she label herself a coach. Instead, she operates at the intersection of identity, behavior, and subconscious architecture — a space she calls emotional engineering."

— CEO Times

"Dr. Channa Bromley stands as one of the most sought-after relationship coaches in the world...Her journey from self-destruction to self-awareness proved that no one is beyond redemption, and that true transformation starts with a commitment to understanding oneself."

— NY Weekly Mag

This book is dedicated to the misunderstood.

To the ones who were condemned before they were guided.

Who were written off before anyone asked what shaped them.

Who were placed in boxes labeled dangerous, disordered, immoral, beyond repair.

To those who made real mistakes.

Who chose actions they later had to reckon with.

Who lived in ways that invited judgment.

And who were still more complex than the worst thing they ever did.

To the ones whose nervous systems adapted under pressure.

Who split because the pain was too much to hold all at once.

Who numbed, hardened, calculated, detached.

Who survived in ways that did not look gentle.

To the people assumed to be lost causes.

Who were managed instead of mentored.

Controlled instead of understood.

Categorized instead of studied.

This book is for you.

It is also for the ones who are willing to look deeper.

For those who refuse to reduce a human being to a diagnosis, a crime, a coping mechanism, or a moment in time.

For the curious.

For the open-minded.

For the ones who can hold complexity without rushing to exile it.

We do not grow by locking people into their worst adaptations.

We grow by understanding what built them, and by guiding what can be integrated next.

No one is helped by condemnation alone.

And no one is defined solely by their damage.

Being misunderstood is not absolution.

But it is not the same thing as being a monster.

Contents

Part Four

Traits, Reclaimed, The Chessboard

Part Five

Responsibility and Choice

Part Six

Reclaiming Humanity

Author's Note

This book is not written to invite identification or comfort. It is written to impose clarity.

It does not ask readers to like sociopathy, excuse harm, or suspend moral judgment. It operates on a different axis entirely. Its purpose is to examine how perception shapes outcome, and how certain ways of naming people quietly increase risk rather than reduce it.

To read this book accurately, a few boundaries must be clear.

I am not writing as a practicing clinician in these pages. This is not a diagnostic manual, a treatment guide, or a therapeutic intervention. I am writing as a strategist and observer of human systems, trained to analyze structure, patterns, incentives, and downstream consequences rather than symptoms alone.

I also write from inside the internal architecture being examined. That position has already been established. It is not a confession and it is not a claim to authority through identity. It is a matter of placement. This analysis is grounded in lived reality rather than abstraction, and it proceeds from responsibility rather than distance.

Nothing in this book argues for tolerance of harm. Harm is harm. Accountability is non negotiable. Explanation does not dilute consequence. If anything, understanding increases responsibility by removing plausible deniability.

What this book rejects is the assumption that immediate moral judgment produces safety.

Much of what is labeled sociopathy is treated as essence rather than adaptation. As what someone is, rather than how certain traits learned to function under specific conditions. That framing feels decisive. It is also inaccurate.

With the exception of psychopathy, which is a distinct construct, sociopathy is widely understood as shaped through environment, injury, neglect, and early relational instability. Biology influences capacity. Experience shapes expression. This distinction matters because it determines whether prevention and regulation are possible.

Villains are rarely born. They are usually produced by unexamined systems.

This does not absolve action. It explains mechanism. And mechanism is where intervention lives.

Cultural morality relies heavily on simplified stories. Heroes are good. Villains are evil. Monsters are different. These narratives create certainty, but they do so by collapsing nuance. They train people to look for labels rather than causes, and to exile rather than intervene.

This book operates differently.

It treats sociopathy not as a moral verdict, but as an internal configuration that can be unconscious or conscious, regulated or unregulated, destructive or contained. It asks what actually changes behavior over time. What reduces harm. What allows responsibility to emerge before damage occurs.

Some of what follows may be uncomfortable. Calm will not always signal safety. Intensity will not always signal care. Emotional restraint may be misread as absence. Emotional expression may be mistaken for depth. These are perceptual habits, not truths.

The aim here is not leniency. It is accuracy.

Accuracy matters because perception is not passive. How people are seen changes how they are treated. How they are treated shapes how they organize themselves. Labels do not merely describe behavior. They interact with it.

This is especially relevant for those who have already been marked as different, difficult, or dangerous. Shame hardens identity. Exile accelerates risk. Understanding, when paired with structure and accountability, creates the conditions for integration.

That is the ethical boundary this book holds.

Compassion does not mean condoning harm. Understanding does not erase consequence. Seeing origin does not absolve outcome. Responsibility remains intact.

What changes is whether responsibility becomes possible early enough to matter.

This book asks to be read with precision rather than sentiment.

If it succeeds, it will not make sociopathy feel safer or scarier. It will make it clearer.

And clarity is where intervention begins.

The Cost of a Word

"The most dangerous thing you can do to a human being is tell them who they are and leave no room for choice."

There is a particular kind of fear that does not come from experience.

It comes from stories.

Most people have never met someone they would describe as a sociopath. Yet the word alone tightens the room. Movies taught us what to imagine. Headlines taught us what to expect. True crime taught us what to fear.

And so a category formed.

A monster.

This book exists because that category is wrong.

Not incomplete. Not exaggerated.

Wrong.

Before we go any further, you should know where this book is written from.

In my twenties, I was formally diagnosed with Antisocial Personality Disorder. ASPD.

I do not lead with this to shock you. I lead with it to remove the illusion of distance. This book is not written from the outside. It is written from inside the internal architecture the word points to.

What that diagnosis described was not my character. It described a pattern of adaptation. A way certain traits organized under pressure. A configuration that could operate unconsciously or be governed with awareness.

At the time, the label meant very little to me. I did not understand the language or its implications. What I understand now is this: a word can name a pattern without explaining a person.

The problem is not that sociopathy is misunderstood.

The problem is that it has been moralized.

A set of traits, behaviors, and adaptations has been collapsed into a conclusion about character. Once that happens, curiosity shuts down. Nuance disappears. Anyone associated with the label becomes something to be watched, avoided, or condemned.

That reaction feels protective.

It is not.

Fear without understanding does not make people safer.

It makes them simpler.

If you are holding this book, something called you here. Maybe someone you love received a diagnosis and you are trying to reconcile the person you know with the word you were given. Maybe you recognize traits in yourself that the world labels as dark, cold, or toxic, and you are tired of being told what that means about you. Or maybe you are simply curious. Uncomfortable with easy villains. Interested in how human behavior actually works.

Whatever brought you here, this book is not an argument for harm. It is not an excuse for cruelty. It is not an attempt to soften reality to make anyone feel better.

It is an attempt to replace fear with accuracy.

Most of what people believe about sociopathy comes from its most extreme expressions. The loudest cases. The least regulated. The people who never learned to contain or govern what they carried. Society then works backward and assumes the diagnosis explains the outcome.

It does not.

Traits are not destiny.

Diagnosis is not character.

Difference is not danger.

What matters, and what has always mattered, is consciousness.

Every human trait exists on a spectrum. Impulsivity. Emotional restraint. Dominance. Detachment. Intensity. Control. In some people, these traits express chaotically. In others, they are integrated, regulated, and deliberately directed. We understand this intuitively in nearly every domain except this one.

We accept that intelligence without ethics can be destructive. That power without restraint can harm. That emotion without regulation can destabilize.

Yet when it comes to sociopathy, we skip the spectrum entirely and jump straight to condemnation.

That shortcut costs us something.

It costs families trying to understand someone they love. It costs people trying to understand themselves. And it costs society the opportunity to prevent harm by addressing the real issue: unmanaged adaptation.

In my professional life, I work as a relationship strategist. I hold a PhD and am trained as a transpersonal counselor. My work places me inside the emotional lives of people navigating attachment, loss, desire, rupture, and repair. Over time, patterns emerge. Not in theory, but in practice.

Traits do not determine outcomes.

Awareness does.

Regulation does.

Ownership does.

This book is written from inside that architecture. Not as a clinician cataloging symptoms. Not as a provocateur performing detachment. But as someone who has spent years studying how traits operate when they are unconscious versus when they are owned.

I am not interested in convincing you that everyone with this diagnosis is safe. That would be dishonest.

I am interested in showing you that the label itself tells you very little about who someone is, how they live, or what they are capable of choosing.

Here is the truth most people avoid.

Many of the traits we fear are the same traits we quietly reward when they appear in more familiar packaging.

Decisiveness.

Emotional restraint.

Calm under pressure.

Strategic thinking.

Reduced sentimentality.

These traits are not inherently pathological. In many contexts, they are admired. In others, they are demonized.

The difference is not the trait.

It is the story we tell about it.

And stories have consequences.

When someone is told, explicitly or implicitly, that they are dangerous by nature, the path forward narrows. Labels that leave no room for agency do not prevent harm.

They accelerate it.

This book takes a different stance.

Not “Are these traits bad?”

But “How do they function when they are conscious?”

Not “Who should we fear?”

But “What actually makes someone unsafe?”

The answers are less satisfying than simple villains. They require abandoning moral shortcuts and confronting a harder truth.

Harm is most often the result of unexamined systems, not inherent evil.

I identify today as high-functioning. That distinction matters.

It means the traits exist, but they are regulated. Choice is present. Responsibility is non-negotiable. I am accountable not only for what I do, but for how I manage what I carry.

This book is not about proving that I am safe.

It is about dismantling the idea that a word can tell you who someone is.

If you are looking for reassurance that all people with this diagnosis are harmless, you will not find it here. If you are looking for permission to excuse harm, you will not find it either.

What you will find is a framework.

One that allows you to see traits without panic. Patterns without moral collapse. People without cages.

The goal is not agreement.

The goal is understanding.

Because once understanding replaces fear, something remarkable happens.

Choice becomes visible again.

And without choice, none of us, diagnosed or not, are particularly safe.

Part One

The Misunderstanding

Chapter 1

What People Think Sociopathy Is

And Why They're Wrong

"When a word becomes a weapon, accuracy is the first casualty."

Most people believe they already know what sociopathy is.

They have seen it in films.

They have heard it dissected in podcasts.

They have watched it dramatized in true crime series that reduce a human being to a single trait and then build an entire narrative around that reduction.

The sociopath, according to culture, is cold, predatory, violent, and inevitable. Someone without conscience. Someone incapable of love. Someone who will eventually destroy everything they touch.

This image feels convincing because it is dramatic. It gives fear a face. It offers a clean explanation for behavior that would otherwise force confrontation with complexity.

And it is wrong.

What most people believe about sociopathy is not the result of careful study or lived proximity. It is the result of repetition. Of storytelling that rewards extremes and punishes nuance. Of narratives designed to provoke reaction rather than understanding.

Once a word enters public consciousness through entertainment rather than education, it stops functioning as a description and starts functioning as a verdict.

That shift has consequences.

When a label becomes a verdict, curiosity shuts down. Differentiation disappears. The person inside the category becomes irrelevant. The word itself carries the meaning, the judgment, and the sentence.

This is how sociopathy became synonymous with violence.

Not because violence is common among people with sociopathic traits, but because violence is narratively efficient. Calm is not. Regulation is not. Stability does not generate clicks.

No one builds a media franchise around the person who goes to work, pays their bills, keeps a small circle, regulates their impulses, and causes no harm. That story does not activate fear, and fear is what keeps audiences engaged.

So sociopathy is taught through edge cases.

The most chaotic.

The most destructive.

The least conscious.

The exception becomes the rule.

The extreme becomes the template.

The loudest story becomes the truth.

This is not education.

It is conditioning.

Repeated exposure to the same narrative trains the nervous system to associate a word with threat, regardless of statistical reality. Over time, the word itself becomes enough to activate suspicion, avoidance, or moral certainty.

Accuracy stops mattering.

Reaction takes over.

Before I ever encountered a diagnosis, I encountered something else.

I learned to read people in environments where misreading them had consequences.

Long before I had language for internal architecture, I moved through spaces where perception was not theoretical. Where intent was rarely stated. Where power was inferred, not announced. Where safety depended on noticing shifts in tone, posture, timing, and desire before they surfaced as action.

I am careful with the word underworld because it invites spectacle. What matters is not the label, but the conditions.

These were environments organized around leverage, hierarchy, appetite, and unspoken rules. Sentimentality was a liability. Naivety was punished. People learned quickly who could be trusted, who could not, and what each person wanted from the exchange.

That training did not come from psychology.

It came from consequence.

In those conditions, behavior tells the truth long before words do. Patterns repeat with precision. Calm can be more dangerous than chaos. Intensity can be performance.

You also learn to regulate yourself.

Not because regulation is virtuous, but because losing control costs you position.

At that stage of my life, those traits were uncontained.

This was low-functioning sociopathy, not because the traits were extreme, but because they were unconscious and ungoverned.

Detachment was efficient.

Novelty regulated me.

People were interchangeable.

Attachment was shallow.

Exit was clean.

Not violent.

Not chaotic.

But unconscious.

The traits operated without reflection, without integration, and without responsibility for downstream impact. Harm was not the goal, but it was possible. Appetite and autonomy were not yet checked by awareness.

That is what low-functioning actually looks like.

I encountered the social verdict shortly after.

I was in my early twenties, working in a strip club, when a woman I had lived with briefly at eighteen approached me. We had not seen each other in years.

By that point, I had made a habit of leaving. The second real connection formed, I disappeared. New city. New environment. New people. Apartments, leases, friendships abandoned.

I did not experience this as loss.

I experienced it as boredom.

Once novelty wore off, I was done.

The longest I stayed under the same roof was maybe six months. The longest I stayed in the same city, two years at most. I could not tolerate stagnation. I needed movement. Distance. Reset.

So when she approached me, I felt exposed before I understood why. Not embarrassed. Defensive.

She did not ease into it.

She told me I was a man eater.

She told me I was a sociopath.

The second word barely registered. It sounded clinical. Abstract. Something that belonged to textbooks or movies.

The first one landed.

I was furious.

Angry at being confronted.

Angry at being accused.

Angry at being reduced to a word in a moment where I already felt on display.

I brushed it off and walked away.

But later, alone, it came back.

Not the word sociopath.

The other one.

Man eater.

In private, without an audience and without defenses, recognition surfaced. Not shame. Accuracy.

Had I hurt people. Yes.

Had I treated men as disposable. Yes.

Had pursuit mattered more than the person. Absolutely.

Once the chase was over, my interest disappeared. Cleanly. Quickly. Without sentiment.

Within a year, I would be formally diagnosed with Antisocial Personality Disorder. ASPD.

The diagnosis meant almost nothing to me at the time. I did not associate it with the word sociopath. I did not pause to integrate it.

I had entered the evaluation hoping to qualify for a paid study. I did not. That was the only part that registered.

It took much longer for those threads to connect.

What mattered in that earlier moment was not whether the accusation was accurate.

What mattered was how the word was used.

Not as context.

Not as understanding.

As judgment.

A single label meant to explain everything and invite nothing further.

That was my first real encounter with sociopathy.

Not as a framework.

Not as a diagnosis.

As a social verdict.

The irony is that many of the traits people fear under this label are the same traits that allow individuals to remain calm under pressure, regulate emotion, and move forward without collapse.

Today, people trust me with their most vulnerable moments. They cry in front of me. They tell me about the ways their wounds created destructive coping mechanisms. They ask me to help them repair relationships they believed were permanently broken.

They do not come to be coddled.

They come for clarity.

That trust does not come from sentimentality.

It comes from stability.

The preference for movement did not disappear with age.

My work is remote. I still move. I still change locations. I still prefer new environments and isolation over comfort and familiarity. I do not like settling. Comfort dulls me. Novelty regulates me.

This is not avoidance.

It is architecture.

Yet these same traits are often pathologized.

People are told they should want more connection, more community, more rootedness. That not wanting these things means something is wrong with them.

This is where fear does its quietest damage.

Not by punishing the extreme, but by shaming the different.

A small subset of the people I work with exhibit clear antisocial or sociopathic traits, diagnosed or not. They struggle not because they are harmful, but because they compare themselves to a model of humanity that was never designed for them.

They are calm.

They are ethical.

They are loyal.

They are productive.

They are regulated.

They simply do not crave social immersion.

They are told that makes them defective.

Sociopathy has become a moral container for everything society does not understand. Emotional restraint. Detachment. Low social appetite. Reduced sentimentality.

Instead of learning how these traits function, we panic.

Fear simplifies.

Understanding complicates.

And complexity is where prevention lives.

Misunderstanding does not prevent harm.

It guarantees it.

What We Get Wrong

- Media rewards extremes, not reality
- Most people with sociopathic traits are not violent
- Labels replace observation
- Fear simplifies what requires precision

Chapter 2

Psychopath, Sociopath, ASPD

Clearing the Fog Without a DSM

"A diagnosis describes patterns of behavior, not the contents of a soul."

Most people use the words psychopath, sociopath, and ASPD as if they mean the same thing.

They do not.

The confusion is understandable. These terms circulate through movies, media, pop psychology, and clinical language that was never designed for public use. Over time, distinctions blurred. What remained was a single impression: dangerous, cold, unchangeable.

That impression is inaccurate.

This chapter is not meant to turn you into a diagnostician. You do not need clinical mastery to understand lived reality. What you need is clarity about what these terms actually describe, and just as importantly, what they do not.

ASPD, or Antisocial Personality Disorder, is a diagnostic umbrella. It is a category created to group certain observable patterns of behavior that tend to cluster together. It does not explain origin. It does not predict outcome. And it does not describe a person's inner world in the way people assume.

ASPD captures patterns such as disregard for social norms, reduced emotional resonance, impulsivity, and difficulty with attachment. It does not tell you why those patterns exist. It does not tell you how they are managed. And it does not tell you who someone will become.

Psychopathy and sociopathy are not formal DSM diagnoses. They are descriptive constructs. Ways of talking about how antisocial traits organize internally and externally.

That distinction matters.

Psychopathy is generally understood as more innate. Research suggests structural and functional differences in brain regions related to fear processing and emotional response. This does not mean choice is absent, and it does not mean behavior is predetermined. It means the starting architecture is different.

Sociopathy, by contrast, is more commonly understood as adaptive. Shaped by environment. Formed in response to instability, neglect, chronic threat, or early relational injury. Less about missing capacity and more about learned containment. Armor that forms early and hardens over time.

These are not rigid categories. There is overlap. There is debate. And many individuals do not fit neatly into either description.

But for lived understanding, the distinction is useful.

One begins with difference.

The other with defense.

ASPD includes both.

Where people get lost is assuming that diagnosis equals outcome. It does not. What actually determines impact is functioning.

Low-functioning presentations dominate public imagination because they are loud, disruptive, and visible. They spill into the environment. They demand attention.

High-functioning presentations rarely do.

In my own life, low-functioning looked like addiction. Cocaine. Alcohol. Constant stimulation. I lived in the underworld, outside conventional rules and expectations. Impulsivity and boredom drove most of my decisions. There was no long-term containment and very little awareness of downstream impact.

There was also calculation.

I used my sex appeal strategically. I understood its effect. I knew it created leverage, softened resistance, and opened doors. At the time, I also believed it was where my value lived. Worth was measured by desirability and reaction.

That was still cognition. But it was not integration.

It relied on external validation and short-term gain rather than internal authority or long-term responsibility. The strategy existed, but it was disconnected from governance.

Low-functioning sociopathy is often mistaken for predatory intelligence. In reality, it is usually disorganized. Reactive. Driven by stimulation and avoidance rather than foresight.

This is where harm is most likely to occur.

High-functioning presentations look very different.

The traits do not disappear. They reorganize.

High-functioning sociopathy is marked by regulation, structure, precision, and awareness. Impulses are contained. Distance becomes intentional rather than chaotic. Ethics emerge not from sentiment, but from clarity.

Consciousness is the dividing line.

In my own life, as awareness developed, functioning shifted. Substance use ended. Chaos settled. The traits that once created instability became tools.

My sense of value moved inward.

I learned that my value did not lie in being desired, but in being clear. Not in provoking emotion, but in remaining stable when others could not. Detachment stopped being a defense and became an asset.

This is why the same traits that frighten people in one context are quietly rewarded in another.

Surgeons benefit from emotional containment. They cannot collapse when a body is open in front of them. Lawyers benefit from detachment and strategic thinking. Executives benefit from decisiveness and tolerance for pressure.

In my work as a relationship strategist and counselor, these traits are functional advantages. I can sit with intense emotion without absorbing it. I can think clearly when others are overwhelmed. I can guide rather than escalate.

This is not a lack of care.

It is a different mode of care.

The problem is not sociopathy.

The problem is unconsciousness.

Society moralizes traits instead of assessing how they are governed.

The same qualities are praised or condemned depending on context, outcome, and narrative.

This is why labels mislead.

The DSM catalogs behavior because behavior is visible. It does not claim to explain motive, depth, or capacity for change. When diagnostic language is treated as identity rather than information, it becomes harmful.

A diagnosis should not function as prophecy.

It should function as data.

The real question is never which word applies.

The question is how the traits are being managed.

Is there awareness?

Is there regulation?

Is there choice?

Without those, any trait can become destructive. With them, even the most feared traits can be integrated into a stable, ethical life.

Precision matters because people are shaped by how we talk about this.

Fear collapses nuance.

Nuance makes responsibility possible.

What We Get Wrong

- ASPD is a diagnostic category, not a personality
- Sociopathy is largely adaptive, not inherently predatory
- High-functioning and low-functioning determine impact more than labels
- Terminology describes patterns, not morality

Chapter 3

Functioning vs Low-Functioning

The Difference That Changes Everything

"The same traits that destroy one life can stabilize another."

The question that actually matters is not whether someone has sociopathic traits.

The question is how those traits are functioning.

This distinction changes everything. Not just theoretically, but practically. The same internal architecture can produce chaos or stability, harm or structure, collapse or leadership. The traits themselves do not determine the outcome. Functioning does.

Low-functioning and high-functioning are not moral categories. They are operational ones. They describe whether a person's traits are running the system, or whether the system has learned to govern the traits.

Low-functioning is not something people simply grow out of. It persists until regulation is learned. It is also what most people recognize, because it is disruptive. It spills into the environment. It creates consequences that demand attention.

High-functioning often goes unnoticed precisely because it does not.

Low-functioning expression is marked by impulsivity without containment. Action without pause. Movement driven by boredom, agitation, or avoidance rather than intention. Decisions are made quickly and lived with later.

This does not always look chaotic on the surface. Low-functioning can appear calculated. Strategic. Even effective in short bursts.

In my own life, low-functioning included calculation. I used what I had. Sex appeal became leverage. Desire became currency. At the time, I believed that was where my value lived.

That belief was not conscious. It was adaptive.

When there is no stable internal sense of worth, value gets outsourced. It attaches to influence, reaction, and stimulation. Whatever reliably creates movement becomes regulation. This can look powerful. It can also be destabilizing.

Low-functioning is not defined by lack of intelligence. It is defined by lack of integration.

There is movement, but no containment. Influence, but no accountability. Action, but no pause.

Impulsivity at this stage is not thrill seeking for its own sake. It is regulation through motion. Boredom is intolerable. Stillness feels like stagnation. The nervous system demands novelty to stay balanced.

This is how people end up in high-risk situations without fully registering danger. The system is not oriented toward self-destruction. It is oriented toward relief.

I paid for many of those decisions. More than once.

But the core pattern was not self-sabotage. It was unexamined momentum.

High-functioning does not eliminate momentum. It disciplines it.

This is where consciousness enters.

Consciousness is not remorse. It is not emotional awakening. It is not self-condemnation or self-forgiveness. It is the capacity to observe pattern without collapsing into it.

The shift is often quiet.

For me, it arrived as a simple recognition. I did not like my life.

Not dramatically. Not with despair. With clarity.

I could see the repetition. The instability following me regardless of city, relationship, or circumstance. I was the common denominator.

That recognition did not come with shame. It came with curiosity.

How does this work?

Why does this keep happening?

What would happen if I learned to manage this differently?

That curiosity changed everything.

Low-functioning traits become high-functioning not through suppression, but through awareness. The traits do not disappear. They reorganize.

Impulsivity becomes decisiveness.

Detachment becomes objectivity.

Reduced sentimentality becomes emotional regulation.

Movement becomes intentional change rather than escape.

The difference is regulation.

High-functioning sociopathy is defined by containment. The ability to pause. To assess. To choose.

Choice is the operative word.

When traits are unconscious, behavior feels inevitable. When traits are conscious, behavior becomes deliberate.

This is where responsibility lives.

Not in feeling bad.

Not in moral self-condemnation.

But in ownership.

Unconscious behavior still causes harm. Lack of awareness does not excuse impact. But awareness creates the possibility of interruption.

This is also where labels do the most damage.

When someone is told they are bad, dangerous, or monstrous as an identity rather than assessed as a system, something subtle happens. The psyche stops resisting the definition. Alternatives disappear.

This is not rebellion.

It is surrender.

Identity becomes fixed. Behavior organizes around expectation. Not because the person wants to cause harm, but because the range of possible selves has been narrowed.

Programming replaces possibility.

High-functioning requires interruption of that programming.

This is why consciousness must be taught as a skill.

The ability to see pattern.

The ability to choose identity.

The ability to design habits and structures that support regulation.

This is not inauthentic. It is architectural.

Every identity is constructed. Some are inherited unconsciously. Others are chosen deliberately.

The belief that identity must be discovered rather than built is a luxury afforded to people whose internal architecture already aligns with social norms. For others, conscious construction is not deception.

It is survival refined into agency.

A monster is a mask.

A regulated, ethical individual is also a mask.

The difference is outcome.

High-functioning sociopathy does not require pretending to be something you are not. It requires choosing how your traits are expressed in the world.

It is the difference between being run by impulse and using impulse as fuel. Between numbness and steadiness. Between chaos and structure.

Society rarely teaches this distinction. It rewards high-functioning traits when they are productive and condemns them when they are disruptive. The same qualities are praised in boardrooms and feared in intimate relationships.

This inconsistency creates confusion and reinforces misattribution.

The truth is simpler.

Traits are neutral.

Expression is not.

Low-functioning creates harm because traits are uncontained.

High-functioning creates stability because traits are integrated.

The difference is not morality.

It is regulation.

And regulation can be learned.

What We Get Wrong

- Functioning determines outcome, not traits
- Impulsivity without regulation creates harm
- Consciousness is a skill, not a feeling
- Integrated traits build structure, not chaos

Part Two

Inside The Experience

Chapter 4

Emotion on Mute is Not Emotionless

How Feeling Actually Works

"Not all silence is absence. Some of it is control."

One of the most persistent myths about sociopathy is that it involves an absence of emotion.

This belief is tidy. It is comforting. It allows people to divide the world into those who feel and those who do not. Those who are human and those who are not.

It is also wrong.

What is often mistaken for emotional emptiness is more accurately described as emotional dampening or apathy. The volume is turned down, not off. Signals still exist, but they do not overwhelm the system, hijack behavior, or demand expression in the way people are accustomed to recognizing as feeling.

This distinction matters because modern culture has confused emotional intensity with emotional authenticity. Loud feeling is treated as real feeling. Quiet feeling is treated as none at all.

In reality, emotion is not binary. It is not something you either possess or lack. It is something that operates differently depending on internal architecture, nervous system regulation, and learned adaptation.

For me, anger is the clearest place to begin.

I feel anger. Strongly. Instinctively. Often with an immediate pull toward correction or retaliation. That impulse is real. It has always been there. What has changed over time is not the presence of anger, but my relationship to it.

In my earlier years, anger was uncontained. It moved quickly from sensation to action. There was little pause, little consideration of consequence, and little awareness of downstream impact. Not because I wanted to cause harm, but because I lacked the internal systems required to slow myself down.

As my consciousness developed, restraint became the skill.

Not suppression.

Not denial.

Restraint.

Today, anger still arises, but it is held. It is observed. It is delayed. I no longer confuse internal experience with permission to act. This is often misread as coldness or indifference.

It is neither.

It is regulation.

Regulation is not the absence of feeling. It is the ability to prevent feeling from becoming damage. This is one of the most misunderstood aspects of sociopathy. People search for remorse as proof of humanity, when what actually prevents harm is containment.

Remorse typically arrives after damage has already occurred. Regulation interrupts behavior before it does.

Empathy is misunderstood in much the same way.

When people talk about empathy, they usually mean emotional resonance. Feeling what another person feels. Absorbing their distress. Becoming flooded by their emotional state.

That is one form of empathy. It is not the only one.

Cognitive empathy functions differently. It involves understanding without absorption. Perception without emotional takeover. Accuracy without collapse.

For me, cognitive empathy is highly developed. I recognize emotional states quickly. I respond appropriately. I take stabilizing action. I say the right things when needed.

Do I feel what they feel? No.

Do I understand what they feel? Yes.

Do I care about the outcome? Yes.

This is where confusion often enters.

If empathy is not emotionally experienced, it is assumed to be fake. Performative. Manipulative.

In reality, it is an interface.

It is a learned relational system that allows me to move through a world designed for emotional expressiveness without causing harm or rupture. I do not use it to deceive. I use it to relate responsibly.

Because it is practiced consistently, it often feels natural. That does not make it false. It makes it functional.

Attachment follows a similar pattern.

I am highly selective. Intensely so.

I experience warmth, loyalty, and protectiveness toward a very small number of people. My siblings. A romantic partner when I choose one. A few rare individuals across my life. The warmth is real, but it is quiet. Subtle. Not consuming.

Spending time with people I care about often requires deliberate initiation. I choose to show up rather than being pulled by instinct. Not because I do not value them, but because my baseline preference is solitude.

Once I am present, I engage fully. I laugh. I listen. I contribute. I want the people I care about to be safe and well. I am loyal once commitment is chosen.

But left to instinct alone, I would still choose solitude.

This is where an important clarification must be made.

This is not loneliness.

Loneliness implies lack. Yearning. Emotional pain caused by absence. I do not experience that. I do not feel empty when alone. I do not miss people in the way others describe.

I thrive in solitude.

My internal world is active, ordered, and sufficient. Solitude regulates me. It sharpens me. It allows my system to remain balanced. Where others become depleted in isolation, I become clearer.

What many people experience as deprivation, I experience as nourishment.

This difference is frequently pathologized because society assumes that social appetite equals emotional health. It does not. It reflects a dominant norm.

Animals occupy a distinct place in this landscape.

My dogs are my primary emotional anchor. With them, there is no interface. No restraint. No translation. The attachment is uncomplicated and safe. Their loyalty is consistent. Their affection is not contingent on narrative, interpretation, or performance.

With animals, I do not manage perception. I do not regulate expression. I do not mask.

This aligns with what we understand about adaptation under instability. When early environments are unpredictable, animals often provide relational safety without complexity. Connection without threat.

This does not mean I cannot care about people. It means trust is earned slowly and selectively, and once earned, it is expressed through action rather than display.

Protection.

Provision.

Reliability.

Consistency.

These are forms of care that are often overlooked because they are not dramatic.

The final misunderstanding to address here is manipulation.

Yes, manipulation is a capacity I possess. So do many people without this diagnosis. The difference is awareness.

Capacity does not equal compulsion.

In my earlier years, I used influence and desirability strategically. I calculated outcomes. I tied my sense of value to reaction. That was low-functioning expression. Effective in the short term. Destabilizing over time.

With awareness came choice.

Today, I recognize influence and deliberately restrain it. Not because I lack ability, but because I care about integrity of outcome. Ethical restraint matters more than advantage.

The greatest frustration many people with sociopathic traits experience is the assumption that they are inherently untrustworthy.

In reality, many are intensely loyal once commitment is chosen. Society often excuses harm when it appears wrapped in emotional expressiveness and condemns restraint when it appears in someone marked as different.

The issue is not sociopathy.

It is unregulated behavior.

Emotion on mute does not mean empty.

Silence does not mean absence.

Selectivity does not mean cruelty.

It means the system works differently.

And different is not defective.

What We Get Wrong

- Feeling is not binary
- Empathy has multiple functional forms
- Selectivity is not a lack of care
- Solitude is not loneliness
- Emotional intensity does not define authenticity
- Regulation, not sentiment, prevents harm

Chapter 5

The Tyranny of "Normal"

Introversion, Difference, and Social Narcissism

"Normal is not the same as healthy. It is simply familiar."

Normal is not a neutral description of how most people behave. It is a social agreement that has been mistaken for truth.

What begins as common preference hardens into expectation. Expectation becomes judgment. Judgment becomes morality. And morality quietly turns into a system of enforcement that rarely recognizes itself as such.

This is how difference stops being descriptive and starts being suspect.

The pressure to be normal almost never arrives as hostility. It arrives as concern. As questions framed as care. As confusion about why someone would not want what others want, value what others value, or respond the way others respond.

The assumption underneath those questions is rarely examined. It is simply absorbed: that shared desire equals health, and that deviation from shared desire must signal absence, threat, or dysfunction.

This assumption is wrong.

Human systems rely heavily on mirroring to feel stable. Shared reactions create cohesion. Shared emotional tempo creates predictability. Shared values reduce uncertainty. When people want the same things in roughly the same way, the system feels safe.

When someone does not participate in that mirroring, the system destabilizes.

That destabilization is not dangerous in itself. But it is uncomfortable. And discomfort invites explanation. Rather than tolerating difference, many people resolve the discomfort by deciding that the difference must be a problem.

This is where normal becomes coercive.

People whose internal regulation does not depend on social approval encounter this pressure early and repeatedly. Not because they are antisocial in the colloquial sense, but because their sense of orientation does not require constant confirmation from others. Their preferences are internally sourced. Their identity is not stabilized through consensus. Their engagement is selective rather than reflexive.

This independence can express itself in many ways.

In some people, it looks like privacy.

In others, dominance.

In others, strategic charm.

In others, emotional restraint.

In others, selective attachment.

The surface expression varies. The underlying structure does not.

The common denominator is autonomy of desire.

Autonomy of desire means that motivation is not governed by shared appetite. Participation is chosen rather than assumed. Validation is not required to maintain internal coherence. Emotional regulation does not rely on constant interpersonal reinforcement.

For systems built on mirroring, this autonomy is unsettling.

The discomfort it creates is often misinterpreted as absence of care. Or lack of feeling. Or moral deficiency. Or danger.

Difference is rarely left as difference.

It is translated.

A person who does not want frequent contact is labeled emotionally unavailable.

A person who does not react visibly is labeled lacking empathy.

A person who does not crave social immersion is labeled disconnected or disordered.

A person who does not mirror enthusiasm is labeled cold, arrogant, or unsafe.

These translations are rarely accurate. They are explanatory shortcuts.

They allow the observer to avoid uncertainty by assigning meaning quickly. They convert ambiguity into judgment. They restore the observer's sense of orientation without requiring genuine understanding.

This is what social narcissism looks like.

Not the obvious kind defined by grandiosity or self-obsession, but the quieter kind that assumes one's own emotional rhythms, desires, and values are universal. It is the inability to tolerate difference without re-centering oneself as the reference point.

Social narcissism does not announce itself as entitlement. It announces itself as concern.

Why do you not want this?

Why does this not matter to you?

Why do you not feel the same way?

Why do you not react like everyone else?

These questions are not neutral. They are attempts to restore sameness. They are efforts to pull the other person back into a shared script so the system can relax.

When sameness cannot be restored, the explanation escalates. Preference becomes pathology. Autonomy becomes diagnosis. The person's internal logic is dismissed in favor of how well they conform to the dominant template.

For people with sociopathic traits, this escalation is particularly familiar. Long before any clinical label is introduced, their differences are already being moralized. Reduced need for emotional reinforcement is mistaken for lack of care. Independence from approval is mistaken for hostility. Emotional restraint is mistaken for absence.

This happens because the culture equates intensity with authenticity and mirroring with connection.

But connection does not require sameness.

Care does not require identical appetite.

Health does not require identical desire.

What the culture often calls intimacy is actually synchronization. When synchronization fails, it is treated as a relational threat rather than a neutral mismatch.

This is where moralization enters quietly.

Difference is no longer simply inconvenient. It becomes unsafe.

Once difference is framed as unsafe, containment feels justified. Pressure increases. The person is encouraged to open up more, share more, feel more, respond more, align more. The stated goal is connection. The actual goal is reassurance.

This process rarely produces insight.

It produces performance.

People learn how to appear normal. They learn when to nod, when to smile, when to react, when to soften, when to withhold. They learn how to simulate engagement in order to reduce friction. The system rewards them for it.

What the system does not do is teach conscious regulation.

Suppression is mistaken for stability. Masking is mistaken for integration. Compliance is mistaken for growth.

This confusion has consequences.

When someone is taught that their natural orientation is unacceptable, but is not taught how to manage it responsibly, they learn to hide rather than understand. They learn to imitate rather than choose. They learn to perform normal rather than integrate difference.

This does not eliminate risk. It delays awareness.

Unintegrated traits do not disappear. They go underground. They emerge later, often under stress, intoxication, power, or emotional rupture. The culture congratulates itself for containment, then expresses shock when suppression fails.

This is not how safety is created.

Safety comes from understanding function, not enforcing form.

Many of the traits punished by the demand for normal are the same traits that provide stability when consciously managed. Emotional restraint. Resistance to emotional contagion. Independence of thought. The ability to remain steady when others escalate. The ability to act without consensus.

These traits become dangerous only when they are unconscious.

The culture rarely makes this distinction. It prefers visible conformity to invisible regulation. It treats sameness as virtue and difference as risk. It assumes that shared appetite equals goodness, and deviation must be corrected.

This approach feels protective. It is not.

Harm is not reduced by forcing people into shapes that do not fit. It is reduced by teaching people how to recognize their architecture, understand its limits, and manage it ethically.

Preference is not pathology.

Not wanting what others want does not automatically signal absence of care.

Not reacting the way others react does not automatically signal absence of feeling.

Not needing the group does not automatically signal hostility toward it.

These conclusions are interpretive leaps driven by insecurity, not evidence.

A secure system can tolerate difference without re-centering itself. An insecure system cannot. It demands sameness to feel safe.

This is the quiet tyranny of normal.

It does not announce itself as cruelty. It announces itself as concern. But its outcome is the same. Difference is punished. Autonomy is mistrusted. And people are trained to doubt themselves long before they ever understand what they carry.

The opposite of normal is not abnormal.

The opposite of normal is specific.

Specificity allows for responsibility. It allows for regulation. It allows for choice. It makes integration possible instead of forcing imitation.

In the next chapter, we move closer to what happens when this cultural impulse to moralize difference becomes clinical. When a word enters the system. When a label is applied. When identity is narrowed instead of clarified.

Before that happens, this distinction must be clear.

Sameness is not safety.

Understanding is.

What We Get Wrong

- Difference is not danger
- Preference is not pathology
- Non-mirroring is not lack of care
- Sameness comforts the insecure
- Autonomy threatens systems built on validation
- Conscious management matters more than conformity

Chapter 6

The Diagnosis

When a Label Found Me

"A diagnosis is not an answer. It is a tool."

Diagnosis is often imagined as a moment of revelation. A scene where language lands with force and identity rearranges itself instantly. A sentence that explains everything.

That fantasy has very little to do with how diagnosis actually works.

When my diagnosis arrived, it did not feel significant. There was no confrontation. No dramatic delivery. No sense of being named, seen, or condemned. No explanation offered and no invitation to reflect.

There was an evaluation. There was paperwork. There was time.

And then there was disqualification.

The context matters, because without it the diagnosis is easily misunderstood.

In my early twenties, I was financially unstable and largely uncontained. I moved frequently. I lived without long-term structure. I worked irregular jobs and gravitated toward environments that rewarded immediacy and intensity. I was using substances. Cocaine. Alcohol. Constant stimulation.

This period of my life was not defined by self-inquiry. It was defined by survival.

I applied to participate in a paid research study because I needed the money. The study involved a multi-day psychological evaluation. I did not see it as personally meaningful. It was a transaction.

The evaluation lasted three days.

It consisted of structured interviews, standardized measures, behavioral assessment, and observation. There was no narrative exploration. No therapeutic framing. No attempt to contextualize my history or inner life. The process was designed to categorize, not to understand.

At the end of the evaluation, I was informed that I did not qualify for the study.

That was the entirety of the interaction.

There was no follow-up conversation. No explanation of implications. No discussion of what the results might mean over time. I was told, in clinical language, that I met criteria for Antisocial Personality Disorder but not the label required for this study (which was Borderline Personality Disorder).

At the time, this information barely registered.

It did not arrive as identity. It did not feel personal. It did not provoke fear, insight, or resistance. It felt administrative. Technical. Abstract.

I was disappointed about the money.

That detail matters because it contradicts a common assumption:

that diagnosis automatically produces self-awareness. It does not. Information without context does not reorganize a life.

The diagnosis existed on paper long before it existed psychologically.

A label does not reorganize a life. Regulation does.

At that stage, I was low-functioning.

Low-functioning is often misunderstood as a moral description. It is not. It is an operational one. It describes the degree to which traits are regulated, integrated, and managed.

Low-functioning does not mean incompetent. It does not mean unintelligent. It does not mean malicious.

It means unregulated.

During that period, my behavior was driven by impulse, novelty, and stimulation. I avoided stillness. I avoided long-term planning. I moved quickly and lived with consequences later. I did not orient toward stability because stability felt dull. I did not orient toward responsibility because responsibility felt constraining.

My nervous system required intensity to feel balanced.

I was not consciously cruel. I was indifferent to impact.

That distinction is critical.

Indifference at that stage was not philosophical. It was functional. I did not experience emotional consequence in real time. Loss did not echo. Harm did not linger. Events passed through without leaving residue.

This is often mistaken for fearlessness or dominance. In reality, it is a lack of containment.

Low-functioning sociopathy is frequently romanticized in culture as predatory intelligence or cold control. In practice, it is usually chaotic. Reactive. Short-sighted. Driven by boredom rather than strategy.

There was no agenda during this period. I was not constructing an identity. I was not using psychology to explain myself. I was not interpreting my behavior through theory.

I was living.

The diagnosis did not interrupt that.

What interrupted it later was not a word, but a shift in functioning.

As my life stabilized, as substance use ended, as my environment became quieter and more contained, something else became possible. Observation.

Patterns emerged. Not emotionally, but structurally. Instability followed me regardless of city, relationship, or circumstance. Similar outcomes repeated. I was the consistent variable.

This recognition did not arrive as shame. It arrived as logistics.

Something in the system required management.

This is when the diagnosis returned, years later, with meaning it did not have before.

By that point, I had education. I had therapeutic training. I had language. I had distance from the chaos that once defined my life. The same diagnostic words landed differently because I was different.

What once felt irrelevant now felt descriptive.

Not as a definition of who I was, but as a map of how certain traits had been operating without containment.

This is the temporal truth most conversations about diagnosis ignore.

Labels do not land once. They land repeatedly across time, and their meaning changes with the person's level of functioning. Information that cannot be integrated at one stage may become clarifying at another.

This is why diagnosis should never be treated as destiny.

Low-functioning is not a fixed state. It is a phase defined by lack of regulation, not lack of capacity. Many people move through it without ever being given tools to understand what is happening internally.

Labels without context do not help. They sit dormant until the person is capable of using them.

In my case, the diagnosis did not explain my humanity. It explained a pattern of adaptation. It helped me understand why certain things regulated me and others destabilized me. Why autonomy mattered more than attachment. Why emotional restraint felt natural rather than forced. Why novelty functioned as regulation rather than escape.

It did not excuse harm.

It did not erase responsibility.

It made responsibility unavoidable.

Once awareness was present, choice became visible. Once choice was visible, accountability followed. The diagnosis did not change my behavior. Consciousness did.

This is the difference between a label and a framework.

A label closes identity. A framework opens responsibility.

This chapter exists to correct a fantasy.

Diagnosis is not a moment of revelation. It is often a delayed explanation that only becomes meaningful when the person is capable of reflection.

That readiness cannot be forced.

What matters is not when the label appears, but when understanding becomes possible.

What We Get Wrong

- Diagnoses often arrive without context
- Low-functioning is not destiny
- Awareness comes later
- Labels land differently over time

Part Three

Moral Imagination

Chapter 7

Villains, Princesses, and the Birth of Empathy

How Moral Stories Teach Us to Misread Humans

"The simplest story is usually the least accurate."

Human beings learn morality through stories long before they learn psychology.

We are taught who is good and who is bad, who is safe and who is dangerous, who deserves protection and who deserves punishment not through data or nuance, but through narrative. These stories simplify the world so children can orient themselves inside it. They teach cause and effect. They teach loyalty and betrayal. They teach right and wrong.

But simplicity comes at a cost.

The earliest moral stories rely on clean categories. Heroes are good. Villains are evil. Princesses are innocent. Monsters are born that way. Motivation is thin. Consequence is obvious. Responsibility is absolute and unexamined.

These stories are efficient.

They are also inaccurate.

As children grow, the stories rarely grow with them. The structure remains intact even as the world becomes more complex. The result is an adult population trained to search for villains rather than causes, and monsters rather than mechanisms.

This is not a failure of intelligence.

It is a failure of moral imagination.

Moral imagination is the capacity to hold complexity without collapsing into certainty. It is the ability to understand origin without excusing outcome. It allows someone to ask how a person became who they are without losing sight of responsibility for what they do.

Most people are not taught this skill.

Instead, they are taught moral sorting.

In moral sorting, characters are divided by outcome rather than process. Harmful behavior becomes proof of inherent badness. Deviance becomes evidence of corruption. Once the label is applied, curiosity ends.

This feels protective.

It is not.

A culture that cannot tolerate complexity cannot prevent harm. It can only react to it.

This is why villains are so often framed as evil rather than adaptive. Evil requires no explanation. Adaptation does.

When someone is framed as evil, the story ends.

When someone is framed as adaptive, the story begins.

This distinction matters because understanding origin is not about sympathy. It is about prevention.

The belief that empathy leads to excuse is one of the most persistent moral errors in modern culture. Empathy is not endorsement. Understanding is not absolution. Explaining a mechanism does not remove accountability.

It increases it.

When behavior is framed as monstrous, responsibility becomes abstract. When behavior is framed as adaptive, responsibility becomes specific.

You can intervene in a mechanism.

You cannot intervene in a myth.

Popular culture has flirted with this distinction, often unintentionally. Some of the most compelling characters in modern storytelling are not heroes, but villains whose origin stories are revealed after the fact. Not to justify what they do, but to explain how they were formed.

The princess who was not saved.

The child who was overlooked.

The outsider who learned to survive without protection.

These characters evoke a different response. Not softness. Recognition.

They introduce the idea that harm often emerges from injury, neglect, abandonment, or misattunement. That biology shapes capacity, but environment shapes expression. That something can be wrong without being chosen.

This idea is dangerous to those who rely on moral certainty.

If villains are made rather than born, then the story implicates systems, not just individuals. Families. Cultures. Institutions. Narratives themselves.

It suggests harm is not an anomaly, but a predictable outcome of unaddressed adaptation.

This is why these stories are resisted.

True crime culture exposes this tension clearly. At its worst, it sensationalizes violence and rewards fear. At its best, it accidentally teaches causality.

When stripped of spectacle, patterns emerge. Chronic instability. Early exposure to harm. Lack of containment. Substance use. Social exile. Unregulated power.

The details change.

The architecture repeats.

The danger is not fascination.

The danger is misinterpretation.

When these stories are consumed without moral imagination, audiences leave with reinforced fear. When they are consumed with a causal lens, audiences leave with questions.

What was missing.

Where intervention failed.

Which signals were ignored.

How the outcome could have been different.

This is the difference between voyeurism and prevention.

Moral imagination does not ask us to feel sorry for harmful behavior. It asks us to stop pretending harm emerges in a vacuum.

One of the most damaging beliefs taught by simplistic moral storytelling is that character is static. That people are either good or bad, safe or dangerous, normal or broken.

This collapses development into essence.

Once essence is assigned, identity follows.

A child labeled difficult begins to act difficult.

A child labeled bad begins to act bad.

A child labeled dangerous learns what is expected.

This is not defiance.

It is programming.

Identity forms through feedback. When behavior is misread and moralized, the response becomes part of the adaptation. Over time, the label becomes more stable than the original behavior that triggered it.

This is where empathy becomes structural rather than sentimental.

Empathy, in this context, is not emotional resonance. It is perceptual accuracy. It is the ability to distinguish between intent and impact, adaptation and malice, capacity and choice.

It allows us to say: this behavior caused harm, and it emerged for reasons that can be understood.

Both statements can be true at the same time.

The failure to hold them simultaneously is what produces monsters.

Late in childhood, I learned this lesson personally.

I was on the monkey bars at school. I was fearless. I liked speed. I liked height. I liked testing limits. I was good at it. Movement felt natural. Momentum felt intuitive.

Another child was on the bars. I do not remember the sequence clearly enough to reconstruct what happened step by step. What I remember clearly is my internal state and what came after.

There was movement. An attempt to direct or demonstrate. Part of me liked being in motion. Part of me liked being in charge.

Then there was a fall.

The outcome was injury.

What followed was not investigation.

It was attribution.

No one asked what I intended. No one paused to assess ambiguity. The conclusion arrived immediately and cleanly. I was reckless. I was aggressive. I was dangerous.

I remember being confused, not because I did not understand that someone was hurt, but because my internal experience did not match the story being told about me.

There had been no malice.

No desire to harm.

There had been movement, momentum, and miscalculation.

What stood out most was not the punishment.

It was the reaction to my affect.

I did not cry. I did not panic. I did not perform distress in the way adults expected. I understood the seriousness. I understood impact. But the expected emotional signal did not arrive on schedule.

That absence became evidence.

Because I did not look remorseful, intent was assumed. Because I did not perform guilt, motive was assigned. My internal state was invisible, so the narrative filled in the gaps.

I became the bad one in that moment.

The label stuck.

Adults treated me differently. Other children reacted to me differently. Expectations shifted. A single ambiguous event hardened into a story about who I was.

That moment did not create a criminal. It did not doom me to violence. But it taught me something precise and enduring.

That explanation does not matter once a story satisfies moral certainty.

That intent is often inferred from emotion rather than evidence.

That being misread can be more formative than being wrong.

This is how children learn who they are allowed to be.

Not through introspection.

Through attribution.

This is why moral imagination matters so early.

When a culture cannot tolerate ambiguity, it resolves it through certainty. When certainty is wrong, it programs error into identity development. Over time, that error compounds.

A child who learns they are bad stops trying to be good.

A child who learns they are dangerous stops expecting understanding.

A child who learns they are other learns to survive without belonging.

None of this excuses harm.

It explains how harm becomes more likely.

Empathy, correctly understood, is not about rescuing villains. It is about interrupting the machinery that produces them.

When we understand origin, we gain leverage. When we refuse to understand, repetition remains intact.

This chapter is not an argument for softness.

It is an argument for accuracy.

The simplest story is rarely the safest one. Clean villains make for satisfying narratives. They do nothing for prevention.

Moral imagination allows us to hold two truths at once. That people are responsible for what they do. And that how they came to be matters if we want different outcomes.

Without this capacity, every deviation becomes a threat. Every threat becomes a monster.

And monsters are very easy to exile.

What We Get Wrong

- Empathy is not endorsement
- Origin is not excuse
- Moral certainty blocks prevention
- Stories train perception, and perception shapes outcomes

Chapter 8

The Architecture of Survival

Why Sociopathy Forms

"What looks like coldness is often the result of heat that never stopped."

Before we can talk about responsibility, we have to be honest about origin.

Not moral origin.

Environmental origin.

Sociopathy does not appear spontaneously. It is not a random defect. It does not emerge because someone lacks goodness or chooses harm. It emerges because something in the surrounding atmosphere makes full emotional processing untenable.

This distinction matters.

Much of the cultural fear around sociopathy comes from a fundamental misunderstanding of how the human system adapts under sustained threat. People imagine cruelty where there is often containment. They imagine malice where there was once necessity.

The architecture did not form to harm others.

It formed to preserve coherence.

There are environments where feeling everything is not safe.

Not episodically unsafe. Chronically unsafe.

Environments where emotional expression invites punishment, escalation, or abandonment. Where vulnerability is exploited rather than protected. Where distress does not lead to care, but to more danger.

In those conditions, the nervous system does not collapse.

It reorganizes.

This is not pathology.

It is survival.

Sociopathic traits often emerge in atmospheres with three consistent features.

First, the pain is sustained. Not a single traumatic event, but a pattern. There is no clear end point and no reliable return to safety.

Second, the pain is uncontainable. There is no stable caregiver, structure, or system capable of helping metabolize what is happening. Distress has nowhere to go.

Third, expression is unsafe. Showing fear, sadness, or dependency worsens outcomes. It attracts aggression, ridicule, or withdrawal rather than protection.

When these conditions exist, the psyche adapts by reducing access to affect.

Not because the individual lacks feeling.

But because feeling fully would interfere with survival.

This is why many people endure suffering without reorganizing in this way, while others adapt by narrowing access to emotion. The difference is not strength or weakness. It is atmospheric necessity.

I learned this distinction early, long before I had language for it.

As a child, a stranger attempted to lure me into a vehicle. I did not panic. I did not cry. I registered that something was wrong and told my babysitter calmly what had happened. She took it seriously and contacted the police. At the station, I repeated the account the same way. The officer listened, then turned to my mother and told her I was likely lying.

His reasoning was simple. I was too calm.

A frightened child, he explained, would have shown it. My composure became evidence against me.

What I learned in that moment was not about danger. It was about credibility. That emotional expression, not accuracy, determined whether someone would be believed. That regulation could be mistaken for deception. That the absence of visible fear could invalidate the reality of threat.

That lesson did not make me unsafe.

It taught me that showing less was often safer than showing more.

This is how emotional dampening begins. Not as indifference, but as calibration.

This is not dissociation in the dramatic sense. It is dampening. Volume reduction. Narrowing of bandwidth.

Feeling less becomes functional.

Emotional intensity is not eliminated because it is unwanted. It is constrained because it interferes with survival.

This is where many people get confused.

They assume the absence of visible emotion means the absence of experience. They mistake regulation for emptiness. They mistake emotional restriction for emotional voidness.

What is actually happening is engineering.

Sociopathic traits solve specific problems.

Detachment reduces overwhelm when attachment is unreliable.

Diminished fear allows action in dangerous environments.

Reduced guilt prevents paralysis when no option is clean.

Strategic thinking replaces emotional dependence.

Self reliance becomes mandatory when co regulation is absent.

None of this is gentle.

But it is coherent.

The system learns what it can afford.

If fear leads to freezing, fear is muted.

If grief leads to collapse, grief is shortened.

If attachment leads to danger, attachment is rationed.

This is not a moral failure.

It is optimization under constraint.

Importantly, this architecture does not emerge because pain was absent. It emerges because pain was too present.

The shutdown is not proof of indifference.

It is proof of saturation.

This is why attempts to treat sociopathy as a lack of empathy often fail.

Empathy is not missing. It is deprioritized when it interferes with function. The system selects continuity over comfort.

This is also why sociopathy is often misunderstood as strength.

From the outside, the individual appears calm under pressure. Unflinching. Capable of operating where others freeze. That capacity is real.

But it comes at a cost.

The cost is not humanity.

It is range.

When emotional dampening becomes habitual rather than contextual, flexibility decreases. The system becomes efficient, but narrow. Effective, but rigid.

This is where risk begins to appear.

Not because the adaptation was wrong.

But because it remains unconscious.

An adaptation that is not brought into awareness cannot be governed. A strategy that was once lifesaving can become destabilizing when the environment changes.

The same detachment that allowed survival can later interfere with intimacy.

The same fearlessness that enabled action can later increase exposure to danger.

The same autonomy that prevented collapse can later block support.

This is not betrayal of the original adaptation.

It is context drift.

What once protected the psyche must eventually be managed by it.

This is where responsibility enters the picture, but it does not erase origin.

Understanding why the architecture formed does not excuse harm.

It explains why governance is necessary.

Without this causal clarity, society does something dangerous.

It collapses adaptation into identity.

Instead of asking what the system learned to survive, it declares what the person is. Instead of addressing conditions, it assigns essence.

Labeling becomes destiny.

Once someone is defined by their adaptation, there is no incentive to provide mirrors, structure, or containment. The architecture is treated as fixed rather than functional. Risk is moralized instead of managed.

This is how harm becomes more likely, not less.

A system built to endure threat does not become safer when it is isolated, blamed, or exiled. It becomes more rigid.

The tragedy is not that sociopathy exists.

The tragedy is that its origins are ignored.

When we refuse to acknowledge that this architecture formed to protect something vulnerable, we lose the opportunity to intervene early, provide structure, and reduce risk before harm occurs.

Compassion, in this context, is not softness.

It is accuracy.

To understand the architecture of survival is not to absolve behavior. It is to see clearly what must be governed.

Only when origin is understood can responsibility be meaningful.

Only when adaptation is named can it be managed.

Only when the system is recognized as intelligent can it be asked to change.

What We Get Wrong

- Sociopathy is not the absence of pain, but a response to too much of it
- Emotional dampening is often protective before it becomes destabilizing
- Adaptation is not identity
- Understanding origin strengthens responsibility rather than weakening it

Part Four

Traits, Reclaimed, The Chessboard

Chapter 9

The Traits Everyone Fears

And How They Become Assets

"What matters is not what you can do, but whether you know when not to."

By the time most people encounter traits like detachment, dominance, or emotional restraint, something has already gone wrong.

A relationship has ruptured. A boundary has been crossed. Someone has felt overpowered, dismissed, or destabilized. The trait is named only after damage occurs, and because of that, it becomes fused to the harm it accompanied. The conclusion feels obvious. The trait must be the problem.

This is how traits become moralized.

Instead of asking how a trait was used, people decide what it means. Instead of examining regulation, they condemn capacity. The trait itself becomes evidence of danger, rather than a variable whose expression was unmanaged.

This reflex is understandable. When harm occurs, people want certainty. They want a clean cause. They want to know what to avoid next time. Naming the trait provides that illusion. It simplifies something that was actually complex. It collapses a sequence of choices into a single characteristic and treats that characteristic as destiny.

This book takes a different position.

Traits are not virtues or defects. They are capacities. Ways perception organizes. Ways energy moves. Ways action becomes possible. What determines outcome is not whether a trait exists, but whether it is governed.

This is the logic behind "The Chessboard".

"The Chessboard" is not about gamesmanship or manipulation. It is not about outsmarting others or winning at human interaction. It is a way of describing how power operates inside a human system. On a chessboard, no piece is moral. Each piece has a defined range of movement, a set of constraints, and a specific vulnerability. Power does not make a piece safer. It makes it more consequential.

A piece moved impulsively becomes a liability.

A piece moved with foresight becomes stabilizing.

Psychological traits operate the same way.

Traits give range. They allow certain movements and limit others. They create advantage in some contexts and exposure in others. The danger is not the presence of a powerful piece. The danger is pretending it does not exist, or moving it without awareness of consequence.

When traits function without consciousness, they create exposure. They move too quickly, too forcefully, or without regard for context.

They are driven by impulse, by boredom, by emotional reactivity, or by the need to regulate discomfort through action.

When traits are conscious, they create structure.

They allow timing. They allow restraint. They allow ethical containment.

This distinction matters deeply when discussing sociopathy, because many sociopathic traits involve capacity. The capacity to remain emotionally unhooked. The capacity to lead. The capacity to dominate a room. The capacity to act without sentimentality.

Capacity without consciousness is dangerous.

Capacity with consciousness is stabilizing.

Detachment is one of the traits people fear most, because it is mistaken for absence. Absence of care. Absence of feeling. Absence of humanity.

In reality, detachment is distance. Distance from emotional flooding. Distance from immediacy. Distance from reaction. It is the space between stimulus and response.

When detachment is unconscious, it looks like disappearance. Withdrawal without explanation. Emotional absence that leaves others confused and unanchored. There is no interface, no regulation, no repair. The person simply exits. Others experience this as abandonment or cruelty, and the harm is real.

But the harm does not come from detachment itself. It comes from detachment without governance.

When detachment becomes conscious, it turns into discernment.

Discernment allows someone to pause rather than react. To assess rather than absorb. To decide whether engagement is appropriate rather than reflexive. It allows steadiness in moments where emotional contagion would otherwise escalate the situation.

In my own work, discernment is not abstract. It is operational. I am often the least emotionally reactive person in the room, not because I do not care, but because reaction would destabilize the outcome. When someone is activated, volatile, or spiraling, my distance creates safety. I do not mirror intensity. I do not escalate urgency. I stay present without being overtaken.

This is not absence.

It is containment.

Ambiguity is another trait that is often treated as morally suspect. People equate clarity with honesty and uncertainty with deception. The demand for immediate transparency is framed as a relational good, without regard for whether clarity is actually accurate or premature.

When ambiguity is unconscious, it creates instability. Information is withheld impulsively, often to avoid discomfort or accountability. Others are left guessing, projecting meaning, filling gaps with fear or assumption. Ambiguity becomes a weapon rather than a pause.

When ambiguity becomes conscious, it turns into emotional sovereignty.

Emotional sovereignty allows a person to tolerate uncertainty without rushing to resolve it. It acknowledges that not all information is available at once, and that premature clarity often creates more distortion, not less. It resists the pressure to offer false certainty simply to soothe someone else's anxiety.

Many demands for clarity are not about truth. They are about control. They are attempts to regulate discomfort by forcing resolution. Ambiguity disrupts systems that rely on emotional immediacy to feel safe.

Used consciously, ambiguity is not deception. It is precision.

There are moments where I could resolve uncertainty quickly by saying something definitive, even when it would be inaccurate. I know the relief it would bring. I also know the cost. Sovereignty means waiting until truth is formed, not manufactured.

Control is perhaps the most maligned trait of all. It is immediately associated with coercion, domination, or manipulation.

When control is unconscious, these associations are often justified. Unconscious control seeks to manage others in order to regulate the self. It constricts. It overrides. It invades. It prioritizes outcome over impact.

When control becomes conscious, it transforms into responsibility.

Responsibility is not about forcing outcomes. It is about managing influence. The more capacity a person has, the more carefully that capacity must be handled.

In lived terms, this often looks like restraint. Awareness of leverage paired with refusal to use it impulsively. Choosing long term stability over short term dominance. Choosing not to move a piece simply because you can.

Control does not disappear when it becomes conscious.

It becomes accountable.

Dominance is often conflated with aggression. It is assumed to be inherently predatory or ego driven.

When dominance is unconscious, it asserts itself through intimidation or force. Others experience it as being overridden rather than guided. Power is used to discharge internal tension rather than to stabilize the environment.

When dominance becomes conscious, it turns into leadership.

Leadership is not about submission. It is about direction. It provides clarity when others are overwhelmed. It offers containment when chaos would otherwise spread. Leadership does not announce itself. It stabilizes through consistency.

In relational contexts, leadership often appears as boundary holding. Naming reality. Refusing to outsource authority to emotional volatility. It is not loud. It is steady.

Reduced sentimentality is perhaps the most misunderstood trait of all, because modern culture equates emotional intensity with moral depth.

If emotion is not visible, it is assumed to be absent. If sentimentality is low, care is assumed to be missing.

This assumption is false.

When reduced sentimentality is unconscious, it can look like dismissal. A failure to register emotional impact. A lack of attunement that leaves others feeling unseen.

When reduced sentimentality becomes conscious, it turns into accuracy.

Accuracy allows a person to see clearly without emotional distortion. It prevents over identification. It allows difficult decisions to be made without collapsing into guilt, panic, or avoidance.

Caring does not always look like feeling. Sometimes it looks like seeing clearly enough to act responsibly.

Across all of these traits, the ethical line remains the same.

Capacity is not compulsion.

Having a trait does not mean it must be expressed. Having influence does not entitle someone to use it. Awareness increases responsibility. It does not erase it.

This is where "The Chessboard" becomes ethical rather than dangerous.

It does not excuse harm. It raises the bar. Once traits are known, they must be governed. Consciousness does not soften accountability. It makes it unavoidable.

The mistake is not having power.

The mistake is pretending power does not exist.

Traits are already on the board.

The question is whether they are moved blindly or deliberately.

What We Get Wrong

- Traits are tools, not verdicts
- Conscious use determines impact
- Power without ethics destroys
- Mastery begins with self-knowledge

Chapter 10

People You'd Never Suspect

High-Functioning Sociopathy in Real Life

"The most stable people in the room are often the least dramatic."

If you asked most people to picture a sociopath, they would not describe the individuals who appear in this chapter.

They would not imagine someone reliable. Someone calm. Someone who shows up consistently, keeps their word, and causes very little disruption in the lives around them. They would not picture someone who avoids drama, prefers structure, and lives quietly inside clear personal boundaries.

That image does not match the stories people have been taught to expect.

This mismatch is part of the problem.

One of the most damaging effects of moralized diagnosis is not fear of the extreme, but blindness to the ordinary. When people are trained to associate danger with spectacle, they stop noticing stability. When harm is expected to look chaotic, contained power becomes invisible.

High-functioning sociopathy rarely announces itself. It does not perform its inner architecture. It does not advertise difference. It often passes unnoticed precisely because it does not demand attention.

In my work, I encounter people with sociopathic traits far more often than public narratives would suggest. They do not come asking for labels. They are not seeking permission or absolution. They come because something in their relational life does not add up. They are repeatedly misread. They are told they are cold, distant, arrogant, or emotionally unavailable, despite having no intention to harm and little evidence that they do.

It matters to be precise here.

I am not diagnosing these individuals. I am not assigning clinical identities. I am observing patterns of functioning. Ways of organizing emotion, attachment, and responsibility that consistently diverge from cultural norms while remaining stable, ethical, and contained.

Many of these people are principled. Not emotionally demonstrative, but internally consistent. Their values are not driven by sentiment. They are driven by clarity. They tend to have strong internal rules, not because they fear punishment, but because predictability matters to them.

They are often misunderstood because their care does not look like reassurance.

One man I worked with led a mid-sized organization. He was described by colleagues as intimidating and aloof. Employees complained that he was unapproachable, that he did not celebrate wins enthusiastically enough, and that he did not perform appreciation in the expected ways.

What was rarely mentioned was that turnover on his teams was low. That people were paid on time, every time. That expectations were clear, and boundaries were stable. That when mistakes happened, they were addressed directly, without humiliation or emotional volatility. His calm was interpreted as coldness. His restraint was interpreted as lack of appreciation.

When we examined his internal experience, there was no contempt toward his team. No desire to dominate. What existed was a low tolerance for emotional noise and a high value placed on fairness and efficiency. He assumed others preferred clarity over affirmation because that was what regulated him.

The issue was not malice. It was mismatch.

Another client worked in a caregiving profession, a role culturally associated with warmth and emotional expressiveness. Partners repeatedly told her she was emotionally unavailable. That she did not need them enough. That she seemed fine on her own.

They were correct. She was fine on her own.

What they missed was her loyalty. Once she committed, she did not waver. She did not cheat. She did not play relational games. She did not seek validation outside the relationship. Her attachment was quiet and durable. But because she did not express anxiety, longing, or emotional dependency, her partners assumed she did not care.

She did not experience love as urgency. She experienced it as reliability.

I remember the first time I realized how often calm was being misread as threat. A conversation ended without conflict, without raised voices, without rupture. Later, I was told it felt "chilling." Nothing hostile had occurred. No boundary had been crossed. What unsettled the other person was the absence of emotional escalation they were used to interpreting as engagement. Stability felt unfamiliar, and unfamiliarity was interpreted as danger.

That moment stayed with me because it revealed something simple and uncomfortable. Many people do not recognize regulation when they see it. They recognize intensity.

High-functioning sociopathy often presents this way. As steadiness mistaken for indifference. As selectivity mistaken for arrogance. As restraint mistaken for emotional poverty.

These individuals are rarely discussed because they disrupt the cultural narrative. They do not fit cleanly into hero or villain categories. They are not charismatic manipulators. They are not violent offenders. They are not redemption arcs.

They are simply different.

Difference is uncomfortable when it cannot be moralized.

Many high-functioning individuals with sociopathic traits operate with a strong sense of personal responsibility. They are aware that their traits carry weight. They manage themselves carefully, not because they fear being bad, but because instability is inefficient and harm creates unnecessary consequences.

They are often less impulsive than emotionally expressive individuals, not because they are more virtuous, but because impulsivity destabilizes systems they rely on. They regulate through structure, not catharsis.

Selectivity is another common feature. These individuals tend to be careful about where they invest energy. Social immersion does not regulate them. Solitude does. Predictability does. Routine does.

This selectivity is frequently misinterpreted as judgment. Others assume they feel superior when, in reality, they become saturated more quickly. Emotional intensity drains them. Prolonged social engagement depletes them. Withdrawal is not punishment. It is regulation.

When this difference is misunderstood, conflict follows.

Partners push for more emotional access. Friends demand more disclosure. Workplaces reward constant social signaling and punish quiet competence. Over time, the high-functioning individual learns that being themselves creates friction.

Some adapt by masking. Others retreat further. Neither option creates understanding.

Loyalty is another trait that is often overlooked.

Contrary to popular belief, many people with sociopathic traits are intensely loyal once attachment is chosen. They do not attach easily, but when they do, they tend to stay. They do not seek novelty through people. Boredom is managed through environment, work, or intellectual stimulation, not relational chaos.

This loyalty is rarely recognized because it is not emotionally demonstrative. It does not come with constant reassurance or verbal affirmation. It shows up as consistency. As reliability. As staying when it would be easier to leave.

When harm does occur, it is remembered more vividly because it feels colder.

Emotionally expressive harm is often contextualized as pain. Emotionally restrained harm is contextualized as intent. Tears soften perception. Calm sharpens it. This is not an objective assessment of impact. It is a bias in how humans assign motive.

High-functioning individuals are also often misread as arrogant.

Confidence without apology unsettles people who regulate through approval. Someone who does not seek reassurance, does not over-explain, and does not perform humility can activate insecurity in others. The response is often projection. The calm person becomes the problem.

This does not mean high-functioning individuals are always right. They can be rigid. They can underestimate emotional impact. They can default to logic when attunement is required.

These are issues of calibration, not pathology.

The danger comes when difference is treated as threat.

When people expect sociopathy to look dramatic, they miss the quieter forms entirely. They focus on the outliers and ignore the regulated majority. This creates a distorted map of risk.

The people who cause the most harm are rarely the ones who have learned to manage themselves. They are the ones who have not. They are the ones whose impulses are uncontained, whose insight is limited, whose shame is unresolved.

High-functioning sociopathy does not guarantee ethical behavior. But it makes ethical behavior possible. It does not make it automatic.

This is the distinction most people refuse to make.

Toward the end of my own low-functioning period, what changed was not the presence of traits, but my relationship to them. Awareness did not make me softer. It made me more accountable. And accountability, not sentiment, is what stabilizes behavior.

If this chapter makes you uncomfortable, that is not accidental.

It is meant to unsettle the assumption that danger is loud, obvious, and dramatic. It is meant to challenge the idea that moral worth can be inferred from emotional tone. It is meant to widen the category of what this can look like in real life.

Because until we can see high-functioning clearly, we will keep mistaking regulation for absence, restraint for cruelty, and difference for threat.

And we will keep missing the real risk factors entirely.

What We Get Wrong

- Functioning sociopathy is more common than people think
- Harm is not inevitable
- Many contribute quietly
- Silence is not absence of ethics

Part Five

Responsibility and Choice

Chapter 11

This Is Not an Excuse

Choice Still Exists

"Understanding yourself increases responsibility. It doesn't erase it."

One of the most common fears people express when discussions of sociopathy move beyond condemnation is simple and visceral.

If we understand it, won't we excuse it.

This fear is not unreasonable. History is full of moments where explanation has been twisted into permission, where context has been used to blur accountability, where understanding has been misused as a shield against consequence. People have learned, often through personal harm, that language can be weaponized. That insight can be turned into insulation. That analysis can become a way to avoid repair.

But the fear rests on a false equation.

It assumes that responsibility depends on ignorance. That accountability requires moral simplicity. That restraint only exists when behavior is misunderstood.

None of that is true.

Understanding yourself does not erase responsibility. It increases it.

This chapter exists to draw a clean line. Not a soft one. Not a negotiable one. A line that holds regardless of diagnosis, history, or internal architecture.

Harm is harm.

It does not become less harmful because someone can explain it. It does not become acceptable because it was adaptive once. It does not dissolve because the person who caused it carries a particular set of traits. Impact exists independent of intention, and consequence exists independent of narrative.

What understanding changes is not whether harm matters. It changes whether harm is inevitable.

When traits are unconscious, behavior often feels compulsory. Impulses move quickly. Reactions feel justified. The individual experiences themselves as being pulled by something rather than choosing. This does not absolve harm, but it does explain why it repeats.

When traits are conscious, that illusion collapses.

Once a person understands how their system works, they can no longer pretend surprise. Awareness removes plausible deniability. It introduces a pause. And in that pause, responsibility lives.

This is why insight raises the bar.

A person who knows they escalate under threat does not get to act surprised when escalation causes damage. A person who knows they detach under pressure does not get to disappear without consequence. A person who knows boredom drives risk does not get to frame recklessness as inevitability.

Knowledge closes exits.

There was a time when I knew exactly what I was doing and chose it anyway. Not because I was unaware, but because restraint felt inconvenient. I understood my patterns. I understood the likely outcome. I acted regardless. The damage that followed was not mysterious, and it was not unavoidable. What was missing was not insight. It was responsibility. That distinction mattered more than any diagnosis ever could.

There are a few phrases that tend to surface when accountability is being avoided. They sound reasonable. They sound self-aware. They are often delivered calmly, even thoughtfully.

I didn't mean to hurt anyone.

That's just how I'm wired.

I didn't feel it the way they did.

I understand now why I reacted that way.

None of these statements negate responsibility.

Intent does not override impact. Wiring does not erase obligation. Emotional experience does not determine ethical consequence. Understanding explains behavior. It does not excuse it.

This distinction becomes especially important in conversations about sociopathy, because many sociopathic traits involve power. Emotional power. Interpersonal power. Strategic power. The ability to detach, decide, dominate, or disengage without internal collapse.

Power is not neutral once it is known.

The moment someone becomes aware that their traits carry weight, responsibility becomes unavoidable. Influence creates obligation. Capacity demands governance. The more range a person has, the more carefully that range must be managed.

This is where many people stumble.

They want the relief of understanding without the burden of restraint. They want explanation to soften consequence. They want empathy without accountability.

This book does not permit that.

If anything, it demands more.

Once traits are named, they must be managed. Once patterns are visible, they must be interrupted. Once influence is acknowledged, it must be restrained when necessary.

Responsibility is not emotional. It is operational.

It is the willingness to regulate behavior even when regulation is inconvenient. To contain impulse even when impulse feels justified. To choose long-term stability over short-term discharge.

Restraint is rarely dramatic. It does not look like transformation. It often looks like nothing happening. A message not sent. A reaction withheld. A confrontation delayed. A decision reconsidered.

But nothing happening can be the most ethical outcome available.

This is especially true for individuals whose internal systems do not generate emotional brakes automatically. When guilt or distress does not rise quickly, regulation must be chosen deliberately. Ethics cannot be outsourced to feeling.

This is not a deficit. It is a responsibility.

Repair sits alongside restraint.

When harm occurs, accountability does not end at acknowledgment. Words alone do not restore safety. Insight alone does not rebuild trust. Repair requires action. Changed behavior. Demonstrated restraint over time.

For individuals with sociopathic traits, repair may feel procedural rather than emotional. It may not be accompanied by visible remorse or emotional flooding. That does not make it less real. What matters is consistency.

Consistency is a form of care.

Containment is a form of respect.

Repair also requires tolerating outcomes that are uncomfortable. Apologies may not be accepted. Access may not be restored. Forgiveness is not owed. Accountability does not guarantee reconciliation.

Responsibility means accepting that consequence exists even when intention was absent.

There is also a necessary reckoning with the limits of self-acceptance.

Accepting your traits is stabilizing. Liking yourself is important. But self-acceptance does not mean self-indulgence. It does not mean refusing feedback. It does not mean reframing every boundary as rejection or every consequence as misunderstanding.

A stable identity can tolerate correction.

In fact, it must.

One of the most dangerous moves a person can make after gaining insight is to weaponize it. To use language as insulation. To intellectualize harm instead of repairing it. To explain rather than change.

This is not growth. It is avoidance dressed as sophistication.

Responsibility requires friction.

It requires tolerating discomfort without discharging it onto others. It requires holding tension rather than resolving it through dominance, withdrawal, or dismissal. It requires recognizing that restraint is not suppression, but choice.

What changed for me was not sentiment. It was structure.

I stopped asking whether my reactions were understandable and started asking whether they were acceptable. I stopped measuring myself against intent and started measuring myself against impact.

That shift did not make life easier. It made it cleaner.

This chapter is not a warning to the undiagnosed. It is a boundary addressed to anyone tempted to confuse explanation with permission.

Choice still exists.

It exists even when impulses are strong. It exists even when emotion is muted. It exists even when patterns feel familiar and justification feels easy. The presence of a diagnosis does not remove that choice. Awareness makes it visible.

And once visible, it cannot be unseen.

Ethics are not automatic. They are practiced.

They are built through repetition. Through decisions made when no one is watching. Through restraint exercised without applause. Through repair pursued without guarantee of forgiveness.

This is what prevents harm.

Not fear.

Not exile.

Not labels.

Responsibility.

What We Get Wrong

- Diagnosis is not exemption
- Consciousness demands restraint
- Accountability is non-negotiable
- Ethics are chosen, not automatic

Chapter 12

What Actually Makes Someone Dangerous

And Why Diagnosis Isn't It

"The most dangerous people are not the ones with dark traits. They are the ones with no mirrors."

When people talk about danger, they rarely mean what actually produces harm.

They mean what unsettles them. What feels unfamiliar. What violates their sense of order. Danger becomes an emotional reaction rather than a pattern that can be examined. Fear replaces assessment, and certainty replaces accuracy.

This is how diagnosis becomes a stand-in for risk.

A word is used to do the work of observation. A label is treated as a forecast. Once that happens, attention shifts away from behavior and toward identity, and the most important question is never asked.

What is actually making this situation unsafe?

The answer is almost never diagnosis.

Danger is not a trait.

It is not a category.

It is not a word.

Danger is a configuration.

It emerges when specific elements converge. When insight is absent. When impulses are uncontained. When substances erode regulation. When power exists without restraint. When integration is replaced by labeling and exclusion.

Remove any one of these elements and risk decreases. Combine them, and risk accelerates.

The most reliable predictor of danger is not aggression or diagnosis.

It is lack of insight.

A person who cannot see themselves clearly cannot regulate themselves. Without self-observation, reactions feel justified by default. Patterns repeat automatically. Consequences are externalized. Feedback is interpreted as attack.

This is not defiance.

It is blindness.

When someone lacks mirrors, internal or external, behavior is not chosen. It is enacted. And enacted behavior, especially under pressure, becomes volatile.

This blindness often begins long before anyone is labeled dangerous.

Fear is one of the primary regulatory systems most people rely on. It creates pause. It signals retreat. It teaches avoidance after threat.

But fear does not function uniformly across nervous systems.

In some people, fear registers late or faintly. In others, it does not arrive at all.

When fear fails to signal, risk becomes invisible.

There were periods in my life where physical danger did not produce withdrawal. It produced stimulation. Situations that would have taught most people to leave instead felt engaging. Escalation did not repel me. It narrowed my focus.

This did not make me dangerous to others.

It made me vulnerable to danger myself.

I have never been a threat to other people. But I have been in environments that were extremely dangerous.

In the underworld, danger followed rules. There were codes, hierarchies, and consequences. Risk was explicit. Boundaries were enforced. When someone crossed a line, repercussions made sense within the system.

That clarity felt coherent to me.

Intimate relationships did not follow those rules.

There, volatility was inconsistent. Aggression was personal. Violence was framed as emotion rather than breach. There were no clear signals for when to leave, and my nervous system did not supply them.

I could intellectually recognize risk while remaining somatically unmoved by it.

That mismatch nearly cost me my life.

The danger did not come from cruelty or intent.

It came from a missing signal.

Without fear to interrupt attachment, I stayed where others would have fled. Without somatic alarm, escalation felt familiar rather than urgent. What should have triggered exit instead registered as stimulation.

This is how people die in dangerous relationships.

Not because they want harm.

But because their system does not register threat in time.

Substance use compounds this vulnerability.

Substances do not create danger in isolation. They remove brakes. They shorten time horizons. They increase tolerance for risk precisely when restraint is required.

This is not moral language.

It is mechanical.

Power without regulation is another accelerant.

Power can be physical, emotional, social, financial, or psychological. Any form of influence over another person's stability or outcomes. Power itself is neutral. But when it exists in a system without insight or restraint, harm scales quickly.

The issue is not capacity.

It is governance.

Shame-based social responses and exile make all of this worse.

This is not because shame is internally felt by everyone. Many individuals with sociopathic or antisocial traits do not experience shame in the conventional emotional sense.

The danger lies in the social mechanism.

When people are labeled rather than assessed, curiosity shuts down. Oversight disappears. Support structures withdraw. The person is pushed to the margins, stripped of mirrors and accountability at the same time.

For those who experience shame internally, exile destabilizes regulation.

For those who do not, exile removes constraint.

In both cases, risk increases.

This does not create safety.

It creates isolation.

Social panic amplifies the effect.

Fear drives response. Nuance disappears. Entire categories of people are treated as threats rather than individuals with specific risk profiles. Attention shifts to labels instead of conditions. The appearance of control replaces actual prevention.

This is how real danger slips through unnoticed.

There was a period in my life where the risk configuration was obvious, even though I could not see it then.

High stimulation seeking.

Chronic instability.

Substance use.

Lack of routine.

Minimal external accountability.

Little internal containment.

None of this required a diagnosis to explain. It was a system designed for volatility.

What changed the risk profile was not fear of consequence or moral awakening.

It was structure.

Insight developed slowly, not as emotion, but as pattern recognition. Containment was introduced deliberately. Routines replaced chaos. Substances were removed. External mirrors were added before internal ones fully formed.

As regulation increased, risk decreased.

The traits did not disappear.

The configuration changed.

This is the distinction society refuses to make.

Two people can carry the same traits and produce radically different outcomes depending on how those traits are governed. One may live quietly, ethically, and safely. The other may generate repeated harm or place themselves in lethal situations.

The difference is not diagnosis.

It is system design.

Danger emerges where insight is absent, impulses are unchecked, substances are present, power is unregulated, and exclusion replaces integration.

Remove or regulate those elements, and risk becomes interruptible.

This is why diagnosis is a poor predictor of danger.

Labels do not forecast behavior.

Configurations do.

The people who cause the most damage are rarely the ones who have learned to govern themselves. They are the ones without mirrors, without structure, without interruption between urge and action.

High-functioning sociopathy does not guarantee ethical behavior.

But it makes ethical behavior possible.

Consciousness introduces choice. Structure supports restraint. Integration creates safety.

This is the work of prevention.

Not panic.

Not exile.

Not moral certainty.

Literacy.

The ability to assess risk accurately. To distinguish danger to self from danger to others. To respond proportionally rather than reactively. To build systems that interrupt harm before it escalates.

Diagnosis does not make someone dangerous.

Unconsciousness does.

What We Get Wrong

- Danger comes from configuration, not identity
- Fear absence can increase vulnerability
- Exclusion increases risk
- Structure prevents harm
- Integration protects everyone

Part Six

Reclaiming Humanity

Chapter 13

Not Broken. Not Normal. Not Evil

Just Different

"I don't want to feel like everyone else, and that's not a defect."

By adulthood, most people have learned to measure health by resemblance. A good life is assumed to be one that looks familiar. Social. Relationally centered. Emotionally expressive. Structured around partnership, shared routines, and constant connection.

When a life deviates from that template, concern follows quickly.

Why would someone choose so much time alone?

Why wouldn't they want more intimacy?

Why wouldn't they organize their life around relationships?

These questions are rarely neutral. They are attempts to locate safety through sameness.

But sameness has never been a reliable measure of health.

For me, solitude has never been absence. It has been regulation.

As a child, the environment I lived in was volatile and unpredictable. Emotional states shifted quickly. Signals were inconsistent. The atmosphere required constant vigilance. There was intensity without containment.

Solitude reduced variables.

Time alone allowed my nervous system to settle. It removed the need to monitor, adapt, or brace. It created quiet where clarity could return. Solitude was not withdrawal. It was safety.

That preference did not disappear with age. What changed was my ability to understand it consciously.

As an adult, my life is not small or avoidant. It is full and demanding. I work with people intensively, often forty hours a week, in emotionally complex terrain. I engage socially. I train my body. I participate fully in the world.

And when that engagement ends, I return to solitude deliberately.

I decompress alone. I read. I write. I design. I watch films. I spend time in nature. I play with my dogs. The quiet is not emptiness. It is restoration.

This rhythm works.

It allows me to remain grounded and regulated rather than depleted or reactive. It allows me to show up with clarity rather than emotional residue. It allows me to choose engagement instead of being pulled into it.

This is not avoidance.

It is structure.

I am also highly driven. Work has long been a source of stimulation for me. Focus. Strategy. Intensity. Problem solving. These regulate my system far more reliably than emotional immersion ever has.

This does not mean work is healthier than relationships in some moral sense. It means it is a safer regulator for my architecture.

Left unexamined, this drive can turn into overwork. Awareness does not erase that tendency. It allows me to manage it.

This pattern repeats across domains.

For a long time, I did not apply this same clarity to romantic love.

In love, I bonded quickly. Intensity felt meaningful. Speed felt like connection. I chose partners whose dynamics activated stimulation rather than containment. Those relationships did not make me cruel, but they did destabilize me.

They amplified parts of me that required more structure than those environments provided.

This is not a judgment of my partners.

It is an observation of fit.

Love, in those contexts, was not regulating. It increased volatility. It reduced clarity. It created conditions where restraint required constant effort instead of being supported by the environment.

Eventually, awareness caught up.

I recognized that romantic attachment, as I had been practicing it, was not neutral for my system. It made regulation harder, not easier. And so, I made a choice.

I chose to be alone.

Not as a rejection of love.

Not as fear.

As containment.

At this point in my life, solitude is not a wound. It is a stabilizer. I do not know if that will change. I do not need to decide that now.

Sovereignty includes leaving the future open.

This choice does not contradict my work in relationships.

I guide others in love not by replicating my life, but by understanding systems. My work is not about prescribing identical outcomes. It is about helping people recognize their architecture and pursue goals that fit it.

Some people regulate best through partnership. Others through community. Others through solitude. Stability comes from alignment, not imitation.

This distinction is especially important for people with sociopathic traits.

Peace is often misread as absence. Quiet is assumed to be emptiness. Emotional restraint is assumed to be coldness. Selective attachment is assumed to be dysfunction.

None of that is inherently true.

Self-acceptance stabilizes behavior.

When someone stops fighting their architecture, they stop leaking energy into performance. When they stop performing normal, they gain capacity for conscious regulation. When they stop apologizing for difference, they stop hiding traits that require management.

This is how integration happens.

Not through correction.

Through precision.

Nonconformity still draws attention. It is questioned. It is interpreted. It is often framed as something that should be corrected.

I register those responses without being governed by them.

They no longer determine how I live or what I choose. I know what stabilizes me. I know what destabilizes me. And I act in alignment with that knowledge.

That choice is not rebellion.

It is responsibility.

A life does not have to look normal to be ethical.

It does not have to be relationally centered to be meaningful.

It does not have to mirror the majority to be whole.

It has to be regulated.

I am not broken.

I am not normal.

I am not evil.

I am specific.

And specificity is what allows a system to function without harm.

What We Get Wrong

- Self-acceptance stabilizes behavior
- Difference is not rebellion
- Peace does not require sameness
- Identity can be sovereign

Chapter 14

If We Stop Making Monsters

We Stop Creating Them

"What we fear, we exile. What we exile, we lose control of."

This book has been arguing one thing in different forms from the beginning.

The most damaging mistakes we make are rarely about violence. They are about perception. We confuse traits with intent. We confuse difference with danger. We confuse discomfort with threat. Then we respond to the person in front of us as if they are already what we fear they might become.

That is how monsters get made.

Not in one dramatic moment. In a thousand small ones. The sideways looks. The tightened tone. The suspicion that arrives before evidence. The assumption that a child who does not mirror is a child who does not care. The idea that someone who does not react like the group must be unsafe.

This is not soft language. It is a system description.

When someone is labeled early as bad, difficult, dangerous, broken, or beyond repair, the label does not just describe them. It trains them. It narrows their options. It shapes what adults expect, what peers allow, and what the child believes is possible.

Labeling becomes prophecy.

If you want to understand how this happens, you do not need a villain. You need a child.

I think about a boy often. He is not one person. He is a composite built from patterns I have seen repeated. Quiet. Watchful. Not expressive in the ways adults are trained to call healthy. He does not perform remorse the way teachers expect. He does not chase belonging the way other kids do. He is smart, strategic, selective, and hard to read.

Adults begin to talk about him as if he is already a problem.

They do not say it cruelly. They say it like concern. They say it like protection. They say it like a warning.

Keep an eye on him. Something is off. He lacks empathy.

And because the system believes that story, it starts treating him accordingly. He is monitored more. Corrected faster. Punished more intensely for the same behaviors other children are coached through. His restraint is treated as defiance. His calm is treated as threat. His difference becomes the evidence.

By the time he is ten, he has learned the rule.

He is not being judged by what he did. He is being judged by what people expect he might do.

That is where the turn happens.

Not because the child suddenly becomes evil, but because he becomes exiled from the possibility of being understood. He stops expecting curiosity. He stops offering explanation. He stops attempting to be seen accurately. He learns to survive as whatever the system already decided he is.

This is how labeling becomes a cage.

This is also why the cultural obsession with diagnosis is often misplaced.

Diagnosis is not the primary danger. Unconsciousness is.

The most serious risk factors are not words on paper. They are lack of insight, impulsivity without containment, substance abuse, power without regulation, and social exile that creates nothing but resentment and identity hardening. When a person has no mirrors, no structure, and no safe relational containers, traits can become weapons. Not because traits are evil, but because no one taught governance.

This is where prevention becomes real.

Prevention is not fear. It is relationship.

Prevention is a competent adult who can sit with a child who feels numb and still teach responsibility. It is someone who can hold space without romanticizing, without shaming, without turning difference into threat. It is a stable human system that stays close enough to teach self mastery before chaos becomes identity.

This is why I built The Rogue Rise.

The Rogue Rise is my project. It is not a brand extension. It is not a charity storyline. It is the applied conclusion of this book.

The mission is simple: we mentor at risk youth through conversation, emotional mastery, and real human connection.

But the deeper goal is structural. We are not just mentoring kids. We are shifting systems by building an army of mentors who know how to create safety, hold space, and spark transformation through presence, not performance.

The Rogue Rise exists for the youth who have already been labeled bad. The youth who are sitting near the edge of outcomes that change a life permanently. Youth pulled toward crime, gangs, prostitution, drugs, and emotional neglect. Youth who have learned that adults do not see them accurately, so they stop offering themselves to be seen at all.

A human can survive a lot.

What they do not survive cleanly is being treated like a monster before they have done monstrous things.

The Rogue Rise is built on one belief: when the most overlooked youth discover their voice, they do not just change their future. They expand what is possible for all of us.

This is the through-line of the entire book.

If perception is intervention, then mentorship is one of the most powerful interventions available.

Not mentorship as inspiration. Mentorship as containment.

The work is not to make these kids normal. It is to make them conscious. To give them language for their internal architecture. To teach them regulation before they build identity around dysregulation. To make choice visible while choice still exists.

That is why The Rogue Rise needs the right kind of volunteers.

Not saviors. Not sentimental rescuers. Not people who need a child's pain to validate their own goodness.

We need mentors with coaching experience, or people who have turned scars into structure, pain into power, and volatility into discipline. People willing to show up consistently. People who can be present with hard stories without flinching, and who can challenge without humiliating. People who can hold a line and still hold a human.

If you read this book and recognized yourself, not in the sensational version of sociopathy, but in the quieter version, the governed version, the responsible version, then you already understand why this matters.

If you can see traits without moral panic, you can see a child without writing their ending.

That is the point.

We stop creating monsters when we stop treating difference like a threat and start treating consciousness like the goal.

The Rogue Rise is where that becomes real in the world, not just on the page.

For anyone who wants to learn more or get involved, the project lives here:

https://www.drchanna.com/theroguerise

What We Get Wrong

- Integration prevents harm
- Community matters
- Labels shape futures
- Choice must remain visible

Chapter 15

What Actually Produces Harm

And Why We Keep Missing It

"Harm is rarely caused by what exists.
It is caused by what is left unmanaged."

When people talk about danger, they tend to ask the wrong question.

They ask *who* instead of *how*.

Who is unsafe?

Who should be feared?

Who carries the trait, the diagnosis, the label that explains the risk?

This way of thinking feels protective. It offers certainty. It creates distance. It allows people to believe that harm can be avoided by identifying the right kind of person and keeping them separate.

But harm does not operate that way.

Harm is not a personality. It is not a diagnosis. It is not a word. Harm is a configuration. It emerges when specific elements converge and remain unmanaged over time.

Traits exist everywhere. Power exists everywhere. Capacity exists everywhere. What determines whether harm occurs is not the presence of these elements, but whether they are regulated, reflected upon, and contained within systems that allow feedback.

When identity becomes the target, management disappears.

Labels feel decisive, but they do not regulate behavior. They do not introduce mirrors. They do not create accountability. In many cases, they remove it. Once someone is treated as inevitable, there is nothing left to examine. The story is already written.

This is why identity-based fear fails as a safety strategy.

Harm increases when traits operate without awareness. When intensity is uncontained. When detachment is unexamined. When dominance meets stress without inhibition. When substances erode regulation. When shame blocks reflection. When feedback is rejected or never introduced.

These conditions are not rare. They are human. They exist across diagnoses, across personalities, across social roles. They appear in people who would never be described as sociopathic and are often excused when they wear familiar faces.

What matters is not whether traits are present, but whether they are governed.

Fear interferes with this process.

Fear simplifies. It collapses nuance. It replaces assessment with avoidance. Moral panic feels like action, but it removes the very mechanisms that prevent harm. When people are exiled rather than engaged, when they are reduced rather than reflected back to themselves, regulation deteriorates.

Mirrors matter.

People do not regulate what they cannot see. Systems do not correct what they refuse to name. Responsibility does not emerge in environments that treat behavior as fate.

This does not mean harm should be tolerated. Harm is harm. Consequence is consequence. Explanation does not erase responsibility. If anything, understanding increases it. Once mechanisms are visible, accountability becomes unavoidable.

Responsibility is not emotional. It does not require outrage or reassurance. It requires structure. It requires feedback. It requires the preservation of choice.

When inevitability is removed, responsibility becomes possible.

This is the distinction that is most often lost. Understanding is mistaken for softness. Accuracy is mistaken for leniency. In reality, moral theater does nothing to reduce harm. Structural clarity does.

Responsibility forms when systems are named. When regulation is learned. When power is matched with containment. When mirrors remain intact even under pressure.

This applies to individuals. It applies to families. It applies to institutions.

Harm is rarely the result of what someone is.

It is the result of what no one managed.

If this book has done its work, it has shifted attention away from monsters and toward mechanisms. Away from fear and toward function. Away from certainty and toward responsibility.

Safety does not come from naming villains.

It comes from understanding systems.

That is where prevention lives.

What We Get Wrong

- We treat harm as a personality instead of a configuration
- We confuse naming with managing
- We assume fear increases safety
- We remove mirrors and call it protection
- We look for villains instead of systems

Conclusion

This book was not written to defend sociopathy.

It was written to dismantle a mistake.

The mistake is the belief that danger lives inside traits rather than systems. That harm emerges from identity rather than configuration. That naming something frightening is the same as understanding it.

It is not.

Across these chapters, I have argued for a different literacy. One that distinguishes origin from outcome, capacity from governance, and difference from threat. One that refuses to collapse complexity into moral certainty simply to feel safe.

Sociopathy, like many adaptations, is not inherently ethical or unethical. It is a way a nervous system organizes itself under specific conditions. What determines whether that organization becomes harmful is not the presence of traits, but whether those traits are unconscious, uncontained, and unsupported by structure.

Danger does not come from darkness.

It comes from blindness.

From the absence of mirrors.

From environments that reward impulse without restraint.

From systems that exile rather than regulate.

From narratives that replace assessment with fear.

When people are labeled instead of understood, nothing is prevented. Risk is not reduced. It is merely displaced, hidden until it becomes unmanageable.

This is why moral panic fails. It feels protective, but it does not interrupt harm. It produces certainty where curiosity is required and exile where structure is needed.

Understanding is not indulgence.

Accuracy is not excuse.

And responsibility does not require dehumanization.

In fact, responsibility depends on the opposite.

A system can only be governed once it is seen clearly. A pattern can only be interrupted once it is named precisely. And a person can only be held accountable when they are not reduced to a myth.

I am not offering reassurance.

I am offering orientation.

If this book has done its work, it has shifted where you locate danger. Away from labels and toward configurations. Away from fear and toward function. Away from essence and toward design.

Not everything that is unfamiliar is unsafe.

Not everything that is calm is empty.

Not everything that is different is broken.

Some systems require precision rather than correction.

Some architectures require structure rather than judgment.

Some lives stabilize not through conformity, but through alignment.

This is not an argument for softness.

It is an argument for competence.

A society that wants less harm must learn to see better. To regulate rather than exile. To intervene earlier. To replace moral certainty with functional understanding.

Monsters are easy to name.

They are much harder to prevent.

Prevention begins where myth ends.

And understanding, not fear, is where responsibility actually starts.

About the Author

Channa Bromley is a relationship strategist, writer, and psychological analyst known for her direct, uncompromising work on power, attachment, and identity in modern intimacy.

Her work has been featured in *Business Insider, The New York Times, Cosmopolitan, Oprah Daily*, and other major media outlets for its sharp insight into dating dynamics, emotional labor, and the unseen structures that govern romantic choice. She is widely recognized for challenging conventional relationship advice that prioritizes reassurance over accountability and communication over discernment.

Channa's approach, which she refers to as emotional engineering, focuses on the internal architecture that drives attraction, tolerance, and repetition in love. Rather than offering platitudes or healing narratives, she works with high-functioning women who understand their patterns intellectually but continue to reenact them emotionally. Her work emphasizes perception over projection, selection over effort, and self-command over endurance.

She holds a doctorate in transpersonal counseling, though she credits much of her expertise to lived experience, high-stakes observation, and over two decades of working closely with clients across cultures, attachment styles, and relational histories. Her philosophy was not formed in abstraction, but earned through real-world pattern recognition and sustained application.

Channa works privately with a limited number of clients and is known for a style that is precise, psychologically rigorous, and deliberately disruptive. Her work is not designed to comfort, but to clarify. Not to validate stories, but to change outcomes.

This book reflects her core belief: that what is labeled dangerous is often simply misunderstood. Not a Monster was written to challenge moral simplifications and to reveal the internal architecture beneath behavior, where adaptation, not evil, is most often found. It invites readers to look beyond labels, to replace condemnation with precision, and to recognize that clarity is what makes conscious choice and self-direction possible